PIANO • VOCAL • GUITAR

THE Doo·Wop SONGBOOK

W9-CHJ-716

A Joint Publication of:

THE GOODMAN GROUP

Music Publishers
New York, New York

and

Hal Leonard Publishing Corporation

7777 West Bluemound Road P.O. Box 13819 Milwaukee, WI 53213

WHAT IS Doo·Wop?

Doo-wop was a style of vocal rock & roll popular in the 1950's and early 1960's. It was essentially an **a cappella** (or nearly **a cappella**) type of close-harmony singing by groups usually consisting of four or five members.

The term "doo-wop" derives from the typical phonetic or nonsense syllables (like "shoo-be-do," "da-doo-ron-ron" or "do-wah-diddy") that were used in the music's intricate vocal arrangements. Background singers used these syllables sometimes as a sort of vocal rhythm instrument, at times just to accent or punctuate the chord changes. The origins of the style can be detected in barbershop quartet singing, and in the music of such black vocal groups as The Ink Spots in the 1930's and the Orioles in the late 1940's.

Doo-wop originated with black urban groups but it was soon picked up by white groups. The first classic doo-wop singles were recorded by black groups in 1954 — "Earth Angel" by the Penguins and "Sh-Boom" by the Chords. In both cases, a white quartet, the Crew-Cuts, did cover versions of the songs and made them into popular radio hits.

Most doo-wop groups sprang out of urban ghettos and were usually formed by friends getting together to sing casually. The Spaniels ("Goodnight, Sweetheart, Goodnight") began as street singers in a Gary, Indiana, ghetto — while the Dells ("Oh, What A Night") started out on street corners in Harvey, Illinois. The members of the Platters (who are represented by five songs in this volume) were working as parking lot attendants in Los Angeles when they met their future manager, Buck Ram, in 1954. Within a year, the smoothly-blending vocal group had a single, "Only You," at #5 on the pop charts. Later they became the first black group to have a number one single, accumulated 40 chart hits overall and became a top nightclub attraction.

The Coasters met in a Los Angeles black ghetto. The often comic foursome enjoyed tremendous success in the late 1950's after it came under the direction of the songwriting team of Jerry Lieber and Mike Stoller. The Drifters' name is apropos — more than 30 different singers passed through this durable group after it was formed in 1953. At the time it recorded the #1 hit "Save The Last Dance For Me," the group featured Ben E. King ("Stand By Me") as its lead singer. The Cadillacs, from Harlem, were known for their flamboyant attire and tight choreography, which foreshadowed the Motown style. The group's biggest hit, "Speedo," was written about their happy-go-lucky lead vocalist, Earl Carroll. Several other doo-wop groups were named after automobiles — the Edsels, the Impalas and the El Dorados all had hit records.

Maurice Williams and the Zodiacs had only one major hit (1960's "Stay"), but it has kept reappearing through the years. The Four Seasons took it to #16 in 1964 and Jackson Browne's version peaked at #20 in 1978. While still in their teens, Little Anthony and the Imperials used singing as a ticket out of their Brooklyn ghetto. The first and biggest of their 19 hits, "Tears On My Pillow," featured the high falsetto of their five-foot four-inch singer, Anthony Gourdine. The Rivingtons, a quartet from Southern California, scored in 1962 with their novelty hit "Papa-Oom-Mow-Mow." In 1981, the group sued the Oak Ridge Boys for copying the phrase in their hit song "Elvira."

The Five Satins recorded their big hit "In The Still Of The Nite" in the basement of a Catholic church while their leader, Fred Parris, was on leave from the Army. Though the song re-entered the Top 100 in 1960 and 1961, the group's history as headliners was short-lived. Louisville, Kentucky was the hometown of Harvey and the Moonglows. The quartet's career took off after radio personality Alan Freed lined up an over-the-phone audition with a record company. One of rock's first racially integrated groups, the Del-Vikings, formed at a Pittsburgh Air Force base. The group scored two top ten hits in 1957, "Come Go With Me" and "Whispering Bells." The Penguins, the Rays, the Silhouettes, the El Dorados, the Edsels and the Monotones were all one-hit groups who never had a successful follow-up.

In the late 1950's, several doo-wop groups gained prominence. Often consisting of Italian-Americans from New York City or Philadephia, their style differed from that of the black groups in that it was closer to Tin Pan Alley than R&B and the lyrics were usually less suggestive (and sometimes pure bubblegum).

The Crests from Brooklyn, were discovered while singing on a subway. Their "16 Candles" inspired a popular movie by the same title in the 1980's. Dion and the Belmonts, Bronx gangmembers named after Belmont Avenue in their rough neighborhood enjoyed several big hits including "Teenager in Love." Dion (DiMussi) later had a successful solo career, kicked his long-standing heroin addiction and became a born-again Christian. During a 20-year career, Frankie Valli and the Four Seasons sold more than 80 million records, easily making them the most successful and long-lived white doo-wop group. The Newark, New Jersey, ensemble (named after a Jersey bowling alley/cocktail lounge) had more than 40 chart hits which featured Valli's trademark falsetto. Danny and the Juniors hailed from Philadelphia. Their saxophonist, Lenny Baker, later co-founded the successful nostalgia act Sha Na Na, but leader Danny Rapp tragically committed suicide in 1983.

Girl doo-wop groups made their mark in the early 1960's. The Crystals, a group of Brooklyn schoolgirls who projected a sultry image and were produced by Phil Spector, recorded a four-million seller in 1963, "Da Doo Ron Ron." The Dixie Cups, a trio from New Orleans, reached the top of the charts during the midst of the "British Invasion" in 1964 with "Chapel of Love," but the group soon faded out. With "My Boyfriend's Back," the New Jersey trio The Angels became the first white girl group ever to have a number one record.

The popularity of Doo-wop faded with the advent of psychedelia in the mid-1960's. But early in the 1980's, there was renewed interest when several groups (including the Moonglows) made new recordings. Later in the 1980's, the Canadian **a cappella** quartet, the Nylons, attained tremendous popularity with a vocal style that drew heavily from doo-wop.

With its colorful vocal harmonies and fun nonsense syllables, doo-wop celebrated mankind's first musical instrument — the human voice. Doo-wop's freshness and appeal has endured for more than three decades and it will likely endure for many more to come.

In the section titled HANDY TIPS FOR SINGING DOOWOP, you'll find the doo-wop syllables sung in the various parts of the song. There is a definite pattern in most doo-wop music: during the verses of the songs, the lead sings the melody and the rest of the group sings *oos* or *ahs* in tight harmony behind him or her. These *oos* and *ahs* usually fall right on the beat and/or when the chords change.

Singing Doo-Wop

AT MY FRONT DOOR

The El Dorados sneak the doo-wops in with *woos* on the chord changes in the first chorus and verses which increase in movement with each chorus. They sing *womp, womp, diddle dee womp* with vocal improvisation and there's a lead falsetto *aye, aye* improvisation with the group singing background.

BOOK OF LOVE

In the intro and chorus, the Monotones integrate the doo-wops into the song: *Oh, I wonder, wonder, whooom ba do who, who wrote the book of love.* The group sings *who do bop bop* behind the lead in the verse. The arrangement has great drum "punctuation," but terrible drum miking—it's definitely a garage recording.

CHAPEL OF LOVE

The Dixie Cups start with an *a capella* harmony and turn arpeggiated syllables such as *ma-aa-aa-rried,* or *the-a-a-a sun will shine* into their doo-wops.

COME GO WITH ME

Here's the famous Dell-Viking intro:
> *Dum, dum, dum, dum, dummm, dum-be-dubbee,*
> *Dum, dum, dum, dum, dummm, dum-be-dubbee,*
> *Dum, dum, dum, dum, dummm, dum-be-dubbee*
> *Dum-wa, wa, wa, wa, waaa.*

This then counterpoints with bass's *doe, doe's* or *no's* throughout the verses. *Never, never,* etc . is sung as the background in the bridge.

DO WAH DIDDY DIDDY

Manfred Mann's simple doo-wop — *do wah diddy diddy dum diddy doo* — is used as the "punch" at the end of each phrase. This is one of the happiest, most "up" doo-wop tunes, and one of the few British doo-wops.

DUKE OF EARL

Gene Chandler makes wonderful use of the song title as the doo-wop and hook in the intro and then as background in the verses: *Duke, Duke, Duke, Duke of Earl, Duke, Duke, Duke of Earl, Duke, Duke, Duke of Earl, Duke, Duke, Duke of Earl.* In the bridge there are *ahs* on the chord changes with the bass singing *bomp, bomp dada dit* and variations thereof.

EARTH ANGEL

The Penguins sing *ooh, ooh, ooh; wo oh, oh, oh-wah, oh, oh* and various combinations thereof such as *wah, oh, oh, oh; do-do-do-do, do-do-do-doo ohh* behind the verses. And on the bridge are pulsating *ahs. You, you, you* in chord sequence is sung at the end. The song is vocally effective with the minimum of accompaniment — just piano and drums.

GET A JOB

The Silhouettes provide a very wide variety of doo-wops with a super bass part ringing through. In the chorus: *Sha na na na, sha na na na nah, ba doom. Yip, yip, yip, yip, yip, yip, yip, yip; boom, boom, boom, boom, boom, boom, boom, boom — get a job.* Behind the verses: *sha na na na, sha na na na nah, ba doom.* On the bridge: *bip dodoo deda.*

DA DOO RON RON
The Crystals sing *da doo ron ron* as the doo-wops at the end of phrases. Note the basic drum accenting in the rhythm of the *da doo ron rons*. It sounds like a marching band bass drum with an incredible echo and this was before such studio effects were available electronically.

GOODNIGHT, SWEETHEART, GOODNIGHT
The Spaniels punctuate with the bass singing *dit, ditdoe, ditdah* at end of each phrase. The background singers sing *ahs* and *woos* on chord changes on the bridge.

HAPPY, HAPPY BIRTHDAY BABY
The Tune Weavers provide a unique female lead over male harmony; *oos* on the chord changes, some falsetto *oos* in second part of verse as punctuation, and the phrase *do you remember* sung by the bass as a doo-wop on the bridge. Check out the wonderful '50s saxophone — sometimes warm, sometimes dirty.

HARBOR LIGHTS
The Platters version features a pattern of background *oo's* on the chord changes and words drawn out to make them "many-syllabled." The instrumentation is very lush and there are added gimmicks of "harbor" sound effects on the recording.

HEARTS OF STONE
In the Fontane Sisters' version, the group sings the melody while a male background group sings *dooda wat, dooda wada doo*. The song is the most country sounding of this collection.

(I'll Remember) IN THE STILL OF THE NITE
In the Five Satins' version, *shoo dooten shoo dooby doo, shoo dooten shoo dooby doo* is sung four times behind the lead with a *woo* replacing the *doo* in the fourth phrase in the chorus. On the bridge, the phrase *I remember* becomes the doo-wop. The group also sings *do ba doo bah* as background to a saxophone solo.

IT'S IN HIS KISS (The Shoop Shoop Song)
Behind Betty Everett's big voice the group sings *shoop, shoop, shoop* in the hook of the chorus with great effectiveness. The use of the "call and response" form of singing in the verse is equally unique. In the bridge the group sings bell-like *booms* in arpeggios up the scale.

LING TING TONG
The doo-wops as sung by the Five Keys is controversial — some feel it's a drug reference and syllabicate it I *ssmmoke-a-boo-eye-a*. However, breathe fresh air and try *tie somoca boom die a* as the intro and as the hook. *Ahs* are sung on the chord changes in the verses.

(You've Got The) MAGIC TOUCH
The Platters *ooo, ooh* and *oooo, wee, oooh* as punctuation after each phrase in the verses, and sustain the *oh's* throughout. On the bridge, they add *aw ow* to the ends of phrases. The lead singer uses syllables to stretch a word: **I-eye-eye** *didn't know too much* or *here I go reeling,* **oh-oh,** *I'm feeling the glow-***oh-oh.**

MY BOYFRIEND'S BACK
The Angels offer the classic girl group spoken intro. The chorus is very effective with the unison duo singing melody with only percussion accompaniment and the doo-wops as the hook by the group — *hey la hey la, my boyfriend's back.*

OH, WHAT A NIGHT
The Dells have a unique interplay with the falsetto singing with the group as they sing *ahs* on the chord changes. The bass punctuates with *do dododoo* and *do do doo* at the end of the phrases and very subtly throughout.

ONLY YOU (And You Alone)
The Platters are at their smoothest singing *oooo, oooo* on the chord changes and switching to *ahh, ahhh, woo oh oh oh oh* at the end of each verse. There are some stretched syllables, such as *only you-oo-oo.*

OVER THE MOUNTAIN, ACROSS THE SEA

Johnnie and Joe crowd varied sound into this song. Under the melody, the bass sings *oos*, and over these is a falsetto voice singing *oos* and *ahs* that sound like singing on the next street corner. There are doo-wops repeats on key phrases. The song is highlighted by corny recitation of the lyric.

PAPA OM MOW MOW

The Rivingtons' bass sings *papa om mow mow* with a strong "jungle" beat throughout. The rest of the group sings *ahs* on the chord changes and *dit, dit, dit* as punctuation.

POISON IVY

The Coasters sing the verse in their characteristic tight harmony, but in the chorus they stretch the syllables, *Poison I-ve-ee-y*, they sing *ahs* on the chord changes. The last time, the verse is sung *laddle laddle lada* as it fades.

RAG DOLL

The knockout of all falsetto voices, Frankie Valli, sings lead while the Four Seasons chime in in tight harmony on *rag doll*, followed by pure *ahs* on the chord changes throughout.

RAMA LAMA DING DONG

The Edsels sing *rama lama, lama, lama, lama, ding dong; rama lama, lama, lama, lama ding dong* in the intro as well as in the background for the verses. The bass booms in with *bom, bom, boms* at the end of the phrases.

ROCK AND ROLL IS HERE TO STAY

In the intro, the Juniors sing *rock* in arpeggios behind Danny in the lead. They then use *rock, rock, rock* or *rock and roll* as the doo-wop lyric throughout the verses. The prophecy in the lyric is most important. Note the modulation to build excitement and the *Jerry-Lee-Lewis-type* piano riffs. "Bop" and "stroll" were some of the dances of the time.

SAVE THE LAST DANCE FOR ME

The Drifters doo-wop with a slightly Latin beat a la early '60s. The second and third verses use the first lyric as the doo-wops repeating *oh I know, yes I know* and *you can dance* as background. *Ahs* are then sung on chord changes in the chorus, with the background singers repeating the hook slightly off the beat.

SH-BOOM (Life Could Be A Dream)

The cover version by the Crew-Cuts of the original Chords cut has been proclaimed by some as the first true rock and roll song.
Intro: *Hey nonny ding dong, a lang a lang a lang, boom ba doe, ba do ba bob eh.*
Verse: *De ooee ow, Sh boom sh boom,*
Bridge: *Ooo, de ooee ow, dot, dot, dot, dot ah,*
Chorus: *Sh boom, sh boom, ya da da daddle de da,*
Last time: *de ooeeo sh boom sh boom.*

SILHOUETTES

The Ray's musical, yet humorous, version begins with melodic *wahs*. In the verses, the group enters at the end of each phrase to punctuate and sing the last lyric. The chorus uses *silhouettes* as a syncopated call and response in an arpeggiated sequence up and down the scale. Toward the end various *ahs* are sung on chord changes and *bahs* sung in the classic triplet sixteenth note rock piano rhythm add dynamics and excitement.

SIXTEEN CANDLES

Ahs and *oos* on chord changes are sung tastefully by the Crests in smooth arpeggiated or moving scale patterns with leading tones to next chords. Key phrases are repeated as a form of doo-wop.

SMOKE GETS IN YOUR EYES

Here the Platters really extend their syllables scalewise: *they-eh-eh-eh asked me* or *oh-oh-oh-oh-oh I of course.* They also sing the Platter pattern of *ahs* in chord sequence, and at the end of the phrase, an arppegiated *do-do-do, do-do-do-wah.*

SORRY (I Ran All The Way Home)

The Impalas doo-wop *ba-ba, sorry* throughout behind the lead singer. On the bridge, there are various *gumba, gumba, gumbas* and *yeah, yeah, yeahs* at the end of the phrases. There's a large brass section on this recording, including french horns, and doo-wop improvisation on the ending.

SPEEDO

The doo-wop singing by the Cadillacs is like a fine-tuned engine! Throughout the song on all the verses including the sax solo, they continually sing *ba bah do-di-dit,* keeping up an intense rhythm. The bass is amazing, singing *bom, bom, bom* up the scale in the intro, as well as *bom*ing throughout like a string bass. On the bridges, each phrase is followed by *bom bah di-it.*

STAY

The Zodiacs sing a steady *bop, bop bop wa doo choo wa wa* behind Maurice Williams. There's an incredibly strong falsetto singing in the second verse with the same doo wops. Rhythmic *bops* are sung as accompaniment in the bridge.

TEARS ON MY PILLOW

Little Anthony sings heartrendingly, while in the verse the Imperials sing *woh-oh-oh-ohh* on each measure, moving up the scale. On the hook, they sing *woh* then *ah* on each chord change. At the end of the hook comes the characteristic stretched syllables: *pain in my heart for you-oo-ee-oo.*

A TEENAGER IN LOVE

A light bouncy *ooo wah ooo* is sung in the verse and *ahs* in the chorus with tight harmonies.

TEN COMMANDMENTS OF LOVE

Harvey and the Moonglows sing *ahs* and *ohs* on the chord changes. The spoken repeat of the verse lyric by the bass is new here, but heard later in the '60s by some of the girl groups. The song has a classic rock arpeggio piano part.

THIS MAGIC MOMENT

The Drifters' version is filled with strings almost obscuring the vocal *ahs* and *ohs* on the chord changes. *Magic* is sung behind the lead singer when he improvises with *wahs* on the bridges. The Jay and Americans' version has very full instrumentation for a doo-wop tune with guitars that are very strong. *Woo's* are sung in the harmony as it builds to the ending.

TWILIGHT TIME

The Platters doo-wop *ooos* on the chord changes in the first phrase of the verses and *ahs* in the second phrases. They *do do* to resolve the end of the verse and sing *ahs* on the chords of the bridge.

WHISPERING BELLS

Another "up" Dell-Vikings sound features their terrific bass doo-woping *dote, dote de oh — ding, ding, ding* etc. with the group singing various *dings or dongs* in the intro as well as the verses. The bass continues singing *dote, dote, de oh dong* at the end of phrases throughout. In the bridge, the lead falsetto doo-wops an improvised melody with the accompanying *ding dongs.*

GOODNIGHT, SWEETHEART, GOODNIGHT
(GOODNIGHT, IT'S TIME TO GO)

Words and Music by CALVIN CARTER
and JAMES HUDSON

SH-BOOM
(LIFE COULD BE A DREAM)

Words and Music by JAMES KEYES,
CLAUDE FEASTER, CARL FEASTER,
FLOYD F. McRAE and JAMES EDWARDS

AT MY FRONT DOOR

Words and Music by JOHN C. MOORE
and EWART G. ABNER, JR.

EARTH ANGEL

HEARTS OF STONE

Words and Music by EDDY RAY
and RUDY JACKSON

ONLY YOU
(And You Alone)

Words & Music by
BUCK RAM and ANDE RAND

Slowly, with feeling

LING, TING, TONG

Words and Music by
MABEL GODWIN

he would nev-er do ____ wrong.

Bb7

Go on and sing ___ your song, a - Ling __ Ting

1 F

no chord

Tong. 2. And as I looked __ a -

2 F **Bb7** **F**

Tong. _____

(YOU'VE GOT)
THE MAGIC TOUCH

Words and Music by
BUCK RAM

You've got the mag - ic touch, _____ it makes me glow so much; _____ it casts a spell, _____ it rings a bell, the mag - ic touch; _____ Oh, when I

IN THE STILL OF THE NITE

(I'LL REMEMBER)

Words and Music by
FRED PARRIS

31

SPEEDO

Words and Music by
ESTHER NAVARRO

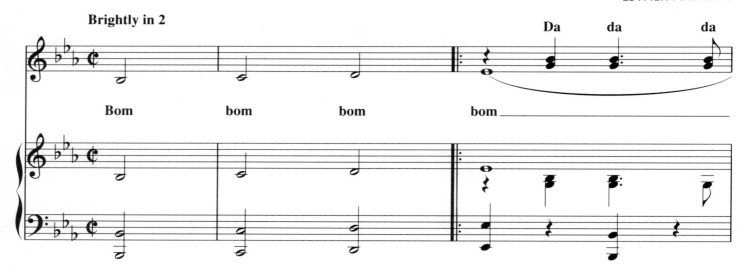

Brightly in 2

Da da da

Bom bom bom bom _____

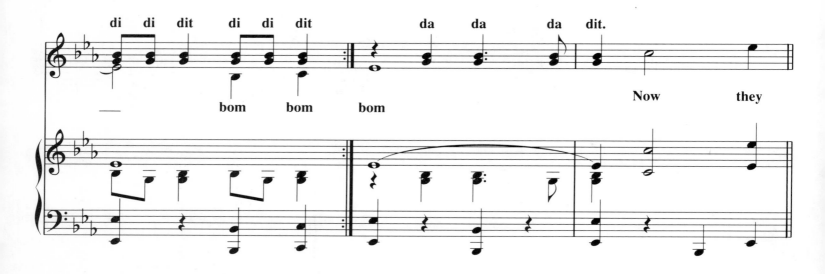

di di dit di di dit da da da dit.

bom bom bom

Now they

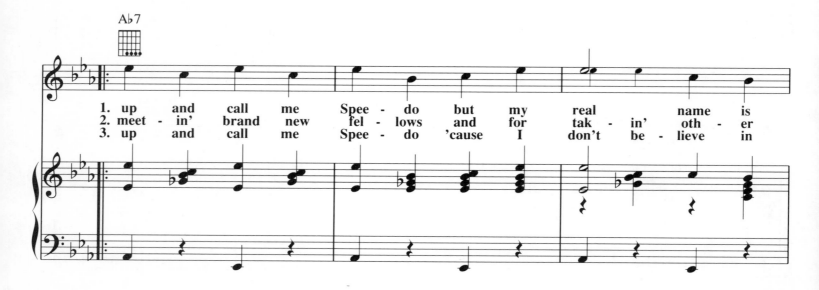

Ab7

1. up and call me Spee-do but my real name is
2. meet-in' brand new fel-lows and for tak-in' oth-er
3. up and call me Spee-do 'cause I don't be-lieve in

OH, WHAT A NIGHT

Words and Music by MARVIN JUNIOR
and JOHN FUNCHES

37

38

COME GO WITH ME

Slow beat

Words and Music by C.E. QUICK

Love, love me, dar - lin', come and go ___ with me, ___ Please don't send me 'way be - yond ___ the sea; ___ I need you, dar - lin', So come go ___ with

41

HAPPY, HAPPY BIRTHDAY BABY

Words and Music by MARGO SYLVIA
and GILBERT LOPEZ

Slow beat

OVER THE MOUNTAIN, ACROSS THE SEA

Words and Music by
REX GARVIN

SILHOUETTES

Words and Music by FRANK C. SLAY JR.
and BOB CREWE

WHISPERING BELLS

Words and Music by F. LOWRY
and C.E. Quick

BOOK OF LOVE

Words and Music by WARREN DAVIS,
GEORGE MALONE AND CHARLES PATRICK

GET A JOB

Words and Music by
THE SILHOUETTES

Moderately, with a rockin' beat

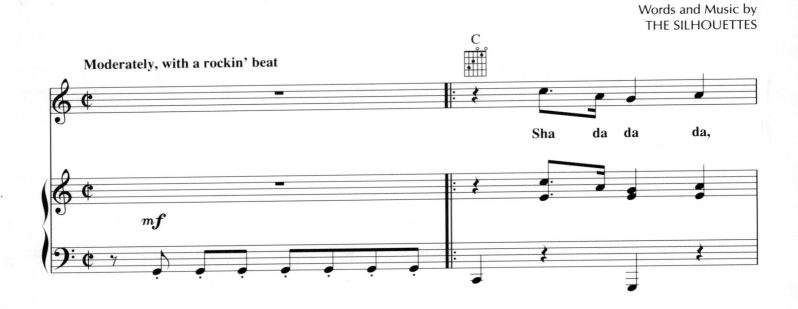

Sha da da da,

sha da da da da,   Sha da da da,   sha da da da da,

Sha da da da,   sha da da da da,   Sha da da da,

58

sha da da da da,   Sha da da da,   sha da da da da,

Yip yip yip yip yip yip yip yip,   Mum mum mum mum mum mum,   Get a

job. Sha da da da,   sha da da da da,   and when I get ___ the ___

pa - per   I   read it through and through   and

ROCK AND ROLL IS HERE TO STAY

Words and Music by
DAVID WHITE

67

SMOKE GETS IN YOUR EYES

Words by OTTO HARBACH
Music by JEROME KERN

THE TEN COMMANDMENTS OF LOVE

Words and Music by
MARSHALL PAUL

TWILIGHT TIME

Lyric by BUCK RAM
Music by MORTY NEVINS & AL NEVINS

TEARS ON MY PILLOW

Words and Music by SYLVESTOR BRADFORD
and AL LEWIS

A TEENAGER IN LOVE

Moderately slow

Words and Music by DOC POMUS
and MORT SHUMAN

Each time we have a quar-rel it al-most breaks my heart,
One day I feel so hap-py; next day I feel so sad.

'Cause I am so a-fraid that we will have to part.
I guess I'll learn to take the good with the bad.

Each night I ask the stars up a-bove:

And if you should say good - bye, I'll still go on lov - ing you.

Each night I ask the stars up a - bove:

Why must I be a teen - ag - er in love, in

love? ____

love? _____

POISON IVY

Words and Music by JERRY LIEBER
and MIKE STOLLER

way it rocks will make you jump and twitch. That rhy-thm's gon-na fool ya, that

slow back beat to cool ya, but poi-son i-vy, Lord, will make you itch. You're

gon-na need an o-cean of cal-o-mine_ lo-tion.

You'll be scratch-in' like a hound_ the

SIXTEEN CANDLES

Words and Music by LUTHER DIXON
and ALLYSON R. KHENT

SORRY
(I RAN ALL THE WAY HOME)

Words and Music by HARRY GIOSASI
and ARTHUR ZWIRN

I ran all the way ___ home

just to say I'm sor - ry.   What can I

HARBOR LIGHTS

Words and Music by
JIMMY KENNEDY and HUGH WILLIAMS

SAVE THE LAST DANCE FOR ME

Words and Music by DOC POMUS
and MORT SHUMAN

STAY

Words and Music by
MAURICE WILLIAMS

THIS MAGIC MOMENT

Words and Music by DOC POMUS
and MORT SHUMAN

RAMA LAMA DING DONG

Words and Music by
GEORGE JONES, JR.

DUKE OF EARL

Moderately with a rock beat

Words and Music by EARL EDWARDS,
EUGENE DIXON and BERNICE WILLIAMS

Da Doo Ron Ron

Words and Music by JEFF BARRY,
ELLIE GREENWICH and PHIL SPECTOR

MY BOYFRIEND'S BACK

Words and Music by ROBERT (BOB) FELDMAN,
GERALD (JERRY) GOLDSTEIN and RICHARD GOTTEHRER

My boy-friend's back, and you're gon-na be in trou-ble.
He's been gone for such a long time.

(Hey, la - di - la, My boy-friend's back)

When you see him com-in', bet-ter
Now he's back and

(Hey, la - di - la, My boy-friend's back)

cut on the dou-ble.
things will be fine.

You're

111

What made you think he'd be-lieve all yours lies?_____ (Ah -

oo_____ Ah - oo) You're a big man now but he'll

cut you down to size!____ (Ah - oo) Wait and see!__ My

boy - friend's back, He's gon - na save my rep - u - ta - tion.

CHAPEL OF LOVE

Words and Music by
PHIL SPECTOR, ELLIE GREENWICH
and JEFF BARRY

Moderato

* Repeat from * to * for fade-out ending

PAPA-OOM-MOW-MOW

Words and Music by AL FRAZIER, CARL WHITE,
TURNER WILSON, JR. and JOHN HARRIS

Pa - pa - pa - pa - pa - pa - pa oom ma mow mow, pa - pa oom mow mow, pa - pa - pa

oom-ma-ma-ma mow, pa-pa oom mow mow, (Doo-doo-doo) oom-ma mow mow, pa-pa

oom mow mow, (Doo-doo-doo) oom-ma-ma-ma-mow, pa-pa oom mow mow.

DO WAH DIDDY DIDDY

Words and Music by JEFF BARRY
and ELLIE GREENWICH

RAG DOLL

Words and Music by BOB CREWE
and BOB GAUDIO

IT'S IN HIS KISS
(THE SHOOP SHOOP SONG)

Words and Music by
RUDY CLARK